Into Fruition

A BOOK OF HOPE, GROWTH, AND WOMEN'S EMPOWERMENT

by

Macellina A. Odd

Copyright © 2022 Macellina A. Odd

All rights reserved. This book or any portion thereof may not be reproduced or used in any manner whatsoever without the express written permission of the publisher except for the use of brief quotations in a book review.

Printed by IngramSpark, in the United States of America.

First printing, 2022

Odd Legacy Joint Ventures
6937 Village Pkwy #2752
Dublin, CA 94568-2405

Into Fruition

In a world full of loud noise, I prefer to be known as a soft sound. There's power in softness. In softness resides peace.

Macellina A. Odd

Introduction:

Dear Friend,
Consider this bounded piece of word art an extended invitation to your next layer of healing.

I've written this book as a dedication to my younger selves, and in turn it has become a dedication to you.

This book, that is me, holds pages of both heartache and pain, of complete joy and affirmation, of worry and trust, of the world and the heavenly realm.

This work is a journey in which I am wholeheartedly inviting you to join me. There will be moments when you feel like I'm reading your mail, moments of "aha" and clarity, moments of connection in knowing you aren't the only one feeling those feelings or thinking those thoughts. Moments of realization that a specific topic applies directly to you.

These pieces are pieces of my heart. Pieces through which I have lived and grown. Pieces that have been broken... and have been healed.

I am inviting you on this journey, a hike if you will, full of trails; to experience the most amazing destination of your authentic self. To lavish on trails of wisdom. It's the trails that hold the wonder, the adventure, the details. It's the trails from which we learn, the ones we experience; and the trails which we are, more than not, most terrified of.

I dare you to take this hike with me! For those who have never experienced this type of adventure before, let me paint a picture of why hiking can become so addictive... even to a brown skinned, loc haired, girly girl, like myself.

In the days leading up to a hike, it's important to hydrate and prepare both mind and body for the strenuous task you're about to endure, and to be open to what the spirit might receive. There is a starting point that is mostly exciting and completely spontaneous. As we begin to climb, however, the altitude rises and so does the amount of effort it takes just to put one foot in front of the other. Muscles start to fatigue and thirst sets in. The majestic mountain that once seemed so distant from the road has become the trail you now follow.

What we couldn't experience before-- the hidden bushes full of berries, the slippery rocks, the various bugs and birds who inhabit that big small space, the fragrance of the flowers so potent it's choking-- all become so incredibly tangible. So real they can seem unreal as the senses adjust and a familiar feeling of present moment takes over completely. Something like Deja vu.

It is within this vibrant place that we can lose our way if not paying close attention. Although alternate paths can present opportunities for excitement, those often-treacherous roads have the potential to lead to grave danger. And after hours of battling resistance and the load of your own weight, your own mistakes, your bad decisions, your heartaches, it is at the peak, the summit on top of that great big mass of earth that we will look over and see how far we have come. Oh, how sweet that moment of deafening silence can be. Like a mouth full of honey. Honey, soothing to the soul.

Fear not Friend! We have a trustworthy guide, a state-of-the-art map, and the final destination is glorious! Would you please... Walk with me?

Into Fruition

To all my contributors,

Those of you ladies who took your time to share heartfelt words of encouragement, knowledge, and wisdom...

"Thank you. I say this because I know you don't hear it enough. You are your own personal strength and the strength of everyone around you. Whether you believe it or not. There is someone that is walking around more hopeful and more inspired just from knowing you. So, I say thank you. Please never doubt for a second that you are anything but love and light."

—*Esther, 21*

Your black girl magic radiates!

Table of Contents

Black Patriot 14

Maci's Mirror 20

As I Open My Eyes 22

QUEEN 26

An Ode to My Hair 42

Woman to Woman 46

Let the Church Say 50

Broken Wings & Healed Hearts: A Testimony 58

Improvisation: A Choreo-Testimony 64

Be YOU 74

What IF? 78

Enough 82

The Journey Through the Chrysalis 84

Six and Counting: Harriet Esi 86

Blankets 98

Into Fruition

Getting the Most Out of these Moments

> Before you begin, close your eyes, and take 3 slow deep breaths.
>
> Take your time. Read 1 page a day.
>
> Read 1 affirmation, the same one, morning and night.
>
> Revisit the same page throughout 1 week.
>
> Read by topic, not necessarily in a linear fashion.
>
> Read with your favorite cup of tea or glass of wine, or whatever you fancy most!
>
> Light a candle or play soft music, create an atmosphere.
>
> Be present. Use this as a meditative moment.
>
> Be open and relax.
>
> Allow yourself to feel the feelings that come.
>
> Write down your responses to the pieces that speak to you the most.
>
> Encourage a friend by sharing something that touched you.
>
> Give yourself permission to indulge in this moment.
>
> Forgive yourself.
>
> Release.

The Hurt...

...it only takes a little bit of trauma to make a lasting negative impact for the rest of our lives.

Into Fruition

The worst disease to have is heartache. It affects every future decision and infects every future potential love interest.

Into Fruition

It's like a crystal staircase.
A porcelain heart in a 4-year-old's hands.
You reap what you sow and if you sow shit,
you reap shit, brotha!
It wasn't as if you had accidentally bumped a
Parisian vase off its mantle.
No! You intentionally picked the vase up and threw
it across the room against the wall and shattered it.
Super glue doesn't work. I used cement paste this time.
Like a ladybug or a newborn child - fragile.
Like the baby hair on my temple frontal lobe.

Black Patriot

Into Fruition

I have been praying, asking God how he wants to use me during this time. A time of unrest and complete chaos. A time that feels upside down. When love is black and hate is white. A time when the American flag creates a visceral effect that makes your heart race and palms sweat underneath clenched fists. A time of global pandemic, climate change, social uproar, and profound income inequality.

Oh, to be a Black woman during this time; hell, during any time.

No one asks us how we feel. How we're doing. What are we doing to cope? They think we have no feelings, no emotions. We can't be hurt...we're Black women.

Who else on the planet...who else in this Divided States of America knows what it feels like to be afraid her husband, her son, and her father won't make it home because a routine traffic stop turned into a modern-day lynching? Who else has fear that outweighs excitement? Second guesses her own maternal choices because she's afraid to give birth to a black son? Afraid because of what THEY might do to him? What they're doing to him before he's even conceived. What they're doing to his mother before she's ever his mother.

Macellina A. Odd

For those of us who bow our heads and take a step backwards, claiming we're not into politics and make no statements of affiliation, I'm here to inform you sistah-girl-friend that everything about you is a political statement...
Your existence is a political statement
Your skin is a political statement
Your hair is a political statement
Your hips are a political statement
So, what statement will you be making?
Is it one of impartiality to humanity?

Into Fruition

The Healing…

…begins with acknowledgement, grows with acceptance, and is complete at surrender.

Into Fruition

The Healing…

The **why** you did that is just as important, if not more so, than the **what** you did.

Maci's Mirror

Into Fruition

Sometimes we just don't know how great we are.
Do you?
Has anybody told you that your food is the sustenance that keeps them going?
Do you know your encouragement has been soothing balm to the weary soul of a friend in need?
Have you delighted yourself to partake in the bounty of your own creations as we have?
You are amazing
You create masterpieces
There is Gold in the hills of your eyes
You are the beauty and the beholder
Sometimes we just don't know how great we are so, when we see each other looking radiant, let's be boisterous in our praises of one another
Let us be loud in our laughter as it runs
Like rivers to the youth we enamored showing them how it's done.
Sometimes we just don't know how great we are because we forgot to look in the mirror and tell ourselves we are phenomenally amazingly making it through the days with grace in our truth that it's hard being born black and a woman, but we do it anyway and we make it look good

—*Shontey Keys*

As I Open My Eyes

Into Fruition

As I open my eyes any given morning, I am reminded…

Someone just got married.

Someone just got divorced.

Someone just gave birth and someone just died.

Someone was just given a clean bill of health.

Someone was just diagnosed with cancer; someone's cancer cell just split for the first time and now their battle begins and they don't even know yet.

Someone just got saved and another rejected God.

Somewhere a tree fell and no one heard it.

Somewhere a miracle happened and somewhere hell just broke loose.

Someone is being raped. Someone is being redeemed.

Someone is being executed for something they did not do.

Someone is being executed for something they did.

Somewhere glass is shattering.

Somewhere the tide is low.

Somewhere it's raining and somewhere the sun is unbearable.

Someone can hear the voice of Satan.

Someone can hear the voice of God.

Somewhere a child is being abandoned.

Macellina A. Odd

Somewhere a barren woman is crying for a baby.
Someone is sneaking a Bible under the covers to learn about Jesus.
Someone is holding a cross in one hand and a pistol in the other.
Somewhere a heart is breaking.
Somewhere a bone is healing.
Someone is making love.
Someone is spreading hate.
All of these and so much more is happening right now in a single moment.

My question to myself is…
What am I doing?

Into Fruition

"To all Black women I will say to you: You exemplify the beautiful graceful spirit of our African ancestors, walking the earth with your head held high no matter what life throws at you. Continue to hold your head high, believe in yourself, don't allow anyone to put you in a box or label you, give yourself grace, don't let anyone dim your light, spoil yourself and allow yourself to be spoiled because you deserve an abundant life. Keep correcting that person who "can't" say your name correctly, don't give in to the pressures of European beauty standards--your beauty is the standard. Keep setting the bar high and use your voice to speak your truth."

—Nkechi Michel

QUEEN

Into Fruition

My Sistah, My Friend... get up and *GLOW!*

Setting *BOUNDARIES* doesn't make you bad. They keep you from being treated that way.

Into Fruition

---   ---

What you choose to do is never just for you.

Macellina A. Odd

------

small in stature,
TALL IN SPIRIT.

Into Fruition

The world will not give it to you; Give yourself permission to rest.

There are a million things you can buy, but show me what is valuable.

Into Fruition

Even when the crown is crooked, it is still in its rightful place. Its honor remains intact.

Macellina A. Odd

I will not allow this world to dictate my decisions any longer.

Into Fruition

---   ---

Go. To. *SLEEP.*

Macellina A. Odd

You don't need anyone to validate you, your *Enough is enough.*

Into Fruition

Learn to get comfortable with things that are uncomfortable.

Macellina A. Odd

Don't put a band-aid on it. Get in there and clean out the wound so healing can begin.

Into Fruition

Things don't have to go according to plan in order to be good.

Into Fruition

"Don't go along to keep the peace. If something violates your conscience or convictions, speak up and take a stand."

—*Sharon Saffold*

An Ode to My Hair

Into Fruition

When you have to schedule time in your calendar for wash day...

Nine years of my sisterlock journey has taught me so much! Patience above all else... endurance...how to accept compliments...

One particular week I was challenged to dress my own wounds (address trauma). Being a woman, a black woman, is a beautifully traumatic and exhausting experience. The insecurity I felt as a little black girl with nappy hair had me worrying how I was ever going to be able to hide my kinky Ghanaian coils from whoever decided to marry me. At 7 years old, that's a BIG thought.

Wearing a scarf to bed couldn't be sexy...even if it is black satin...right?

"What was the first thing you noticed about her?"

Husband: "Her hair."

How do I make room to grow life? I clear out the toxic clutter. I accept my own glory. I lay new foundations of healthier soils. I teach what I've learned...not what I'm ashamed of. Not easy, but necessary.

Frightening yet fascinating. Love. And water.

Two knew me close enough to call me dramatic. One was embarrassed. The other embraced what it truly was... expression. This is the result of that embrace.

Into Fruition

"It's okay to feel our emotions. It's okay to receive love. It's okay to receive a helping hand. It's okay to want/have companionship."

—*Ashley Frazier*

Woman to Woman

Into Fruition

When you don't know where to go, go back to what you know.

YOU are ENOUGH. you ARE enough.

Under promise, over deliver.

I wear my scars as badges.

Stay present, stay gracious, stay grounded.

The closer you look, the more you will find. Make sure you're searching in the right places.

You are not a mistake. You were purposefully created with a purpose to fulfill.

You cannot sow life where death dwells. Let it go.

If you flirt with fire, it is a matter of time before the burn.

There's no such thing as coincidence, only timely orchestration.

It's when you tap into purpose that the whys get answered.

You can't expect more from people than they expect from themselves. You're setting yourself up for disappointment.

Pay attention, search yourself for what brings you to life, and SEIZE it!

I can help you…but I cannot make you…

The degree might make you a professional, but experience will always make you the expert.

Life is a continuous group project with an individual final grade.

Macellina A. Odd

"Develop standards and boundaries for yourself and then stand by them. Don't lower them or compromise them for anyone."

—*Sharon Saffold*

Into Fruition

Psalms 126: 1-5

"Trials and Tribulations can and will come. Sometimes we can feel like we are in the dark so long that we lose sight of God's ability to exceed our expectations. So often we are limited by our own understanding. In the moment of darkness we can't even begin to imagine the blessings coming our way because life's trials and experiences have restricted our ability to see past what's tangible. The expectations we have are typically lower than what God has for us. So, he is patient with us and waits for us to believe and have faith so He can begin the expansion of us, in order to bless us to our capacity.

When our expectations are unmet time after time, disappointment after disappointment, it's easy to become defeated and depressed. We can't let temporary circumstances or trials limit God's capability. 'Don't handicap your blessing because you aren't spiritually ready.' Ask, seek and pray and watch the blessings begin to flow."

—***Leslie Odd***

Let The Church Say...

Into Fruition

---   ---

You wanna see mountains move? Let a child petition prayer on your behalf.
#JourneyKeys

Macellina A. Odd

Pray hard. Work smart. Slay demons.

Into Fruition

You cannot bless and curse from the same vessel. Guard your heart and watch your mouth!

Macellina A. Odd

Thank you, Lord, for the hurt that has led to this harvest. Amen.

Into Fruition

May every Godly ambition come completely into fruition.

Your validation came at the foot of the cross. *ENOUGH.*

Into Fruition

---   ---

"Be willing to listen and learn from everyone and every experience you have in your life."

—*Sharon Saffold*

Broken Wings & Healed Hearts: A Testimony

Into Fruition

This is not intended to be a sad story, but rather a testimony of hope. I am growing to openly embrace my struggle with a disability and as a result, use my "broken wing" as a platform of strength.

"They won't understand if I tell them. How many ways can I find to hide this ugly part of me?" I can't pinpoint the exact time my perception began to change. I do know that there came a time that I got so tired of worrying about it that I stopped caring all together – until I had to tell the "scar story" again. I felt if no one knew then no one would treat me any different. I hid behind long sleeve shirts and sweaters even in the 104-degree Sacramento summer heat. I held my books and my purses in a very particular way in order to make my arm appear "normal"; even though I didn't have any feeling from the knuckle of my pinky finger to the outside middle section of my forearm.

Due to a doctor's oversight, I was injured at birth., I now have a condition known as Erb's Palsy. This condition has forced me to adapt, improvise my entire life. It has shaped my perspective on "correctness" because there are many things I must do, and in order to accomplish daily tasks, I have to approach them in a way that is typically deemed "incorrect". It has made my life both difficult and exciting! I have grown to be both self-conscience and strong-willed. Resiliency abounds out of dark experiences and challenging situations. My life approach is very different from most people close to me. As a child I had to explain why I couldn't do cartwheels or raise both arms above my head in P.E. As an adolescent I had to figure out how to drive keeping both hands at ten-and-two instead of three-and-eight which is naturally more comfortable, given my limitations. As a college student my identity was attacked daily by comparisons of body structures, parallel limbs and the scar-free skin that covered them.

As a thirty-something I have to pause and think about how to hold a child securely. Even in the moments of typing an autobiographical essay for a graduate school application, both sets of fingers do not strike the appropriate keys as they should, based on the tutorials we were graded on in 2001. I had to think harder to keep people from noticing and most of the time it worked. But I noticed. Then one day I found reverence in dance and decided that I didn't care anymore… that is until I could no longer perform extensions properly and I began to think more about how my body looked contorted rather than how I was actually executing the movements. Erb's Palsy is my permanent slice of humble pie. It does not taste good, in fact it's awful. But it was necessary; and it has forced me to thrive.

At the age of six I had an operation that would allow me to properly lift my wrist. At that age, my six-year-old thoughts were that I would be fixed, and everything would be normal like all my friends at school. It was not until the bright pink cast was removed that I met the huge scar that I would spend many years doing my best to hide. Underneath the darkened, deadened skin and weird smelling sweat lied a part of me that I did not understand and, at 32 years of age only began to identify with. Created from this was a perfect battleground for threatening soldiers of insecurity, fear, rejection, low self-esteem, depression and any other negative self-belief you can think of.

As a child I remember often asking my parents, "Why did this happen to me?"

My mother's response was something to the effect of, "God gives all of us a challenge in life, some are easier to see than others and some seem more serious. But He knows each of us better than we know each other, and your challenge is with your arm because you are the only one of us strong enough to handle it." Even as I write this, that explanation brings tears to my eyes. I can only imagine how she must have felt having to explain this to me as her young child. I would assume rather heartbreaking. This is my wing, not easily broken.

Faith has been my lifelong experience. It continues to challenge me in ways that boggle my mind and sharpen my senses. My faith tunes my sensitivity within myself and towards others. I believe without a shadow of doubt that my faith is how I conquer battles of my body and mind. With God I can do all things. With Him I have danced in performances in front of thousands of people who filled the seats of big stadiums and arenas. With Him I have safely reached thousands of destinations as the sole driver of my very own vehicle. My God has lovingly allowed mothers to trust the placement of their most personal and valuable possessions in my arms, their children, who always seem to look up at me and smile, as if they are in on my little secret. With Him I have spoken to crowds of little girls, young ladies, and elderly women who have been broken into a million pieces. Whose physical and mental health was in some type of jeopardy and were desperate to hear a word of truth. This is my wing.

Improvisation: A Choreo-Testimony

Into Fruition

(Matt. 12: 10, 13) And behold, there was a woman with a withered hand…Then He said to the woman, "…stretch out your hand." And she stretched it out and it was restored as whole as the other.

Improvisation defined: To invent, compose, or perform with little or no preparation.

Nothing can prepare us for a broken anything…not a bone, bond, or wing.

Heart.

But over the years I have been given the gift to improvise.

Hmm, where do I start?

I still haven't learned how to do a cartwheel, a six-year old's joy

I was afraid to try it single handed, o'boy. So, I sat… and I watched.

Once, I opened my mouth and started to sing, what I really wanted was to dance,

Even with my broken wing.

So, I stretched out my hands and I started to flow and I started to fly and suddenly thought…

"Oh my… what if someone is watching?"

I kneeled down bedside and worry began to set,

I've gotta find a way to improvise, I'm getting anxious, starting to fret.

Then all these thoughts rushed and took over me,

What if I never learn to drive a car or hold my own baby?

What if one of these Sacramento summers gets so hot that I have to take off my long sleeve hoodie?

Yea, it gets sweaty but the alternative is worse cuz then they'll see the zig-zag scar and I'll have to explain that no, I didn't try to commit suicide and slipped up with the knife!

And no, there was no car accident. I've dealt with this all my life.

What if they ask me questions then don't like my answers?

It might be easier to accept if it was some disease, one of them types of cancers...

I got treated no differently than my brother or sisters, not by begging or wishes,

In my momma's house, "oh you 'gon learn to wash them dishes", so to complete my chore list I was forced to improvise.

What if they notice my free throw is a little off despite my good stamina?

And I haven't seen too many wrist length prom dresses ...

But still I can imagine myself up high on a stage struttin'
Katherine Dunham walks and an Alvin Ailey arm raise…
Flat back in perfect position …It almost makes me forget
my condition.

I can't help but see Martha Graham's extensions.

Beginning jazz professor Ms. Lisa's critique, "Maci, your
lack of confidence affects your performance ability. Relax
and enjoy the movement. Even though your arm hinders
you, the rest of your body should extend fully and expand
out into space" …B+.

Musicality, rhythmic accuracy − excellent.

Concentration, creativity, movement quality − excellent.

Confidence…needs improvement − improvise.

2nd grade improvisation, my momma typed out my 3-page
report on ladybugs. She wasn't available for that task
when I had to fulfill a bachelors' degree requirement at a
university and complete 32 pages on epidemiology--the
study of disease travel.

When I took an interest in cooking, I realized the correct
way to hold a potato in order to peel it wasn't the way I was
holding it and therefore I was forced to improvise.

Try being 13 and "properly" hooking your bra in the gym
class locker room. But I had to get it on and to my 5th

period class so I improvised.

There's a musical in my head where street crossings shout pictures of jazz walks and kick-ball-changes.

Where the look of the eye of a sexy chocolate man invokes haughty exchanges, and his full lips and essence of incense in his locks make my feet cha-cha and my hips all hot.

And after a glass of red wine, I can share with you my friend an intricate jazz square.

I plie' in my cubicle and fan kick in my bedroom.

My feet position themselves in turnout while I'm in the shower, not on purpose of course!

Nothing expresses my soul like that of a body roll

And I've learned to Samba a room wild!

Sometimes deep inside I hear the voice of my inner child… smiling.

Though once I was too afraid to examine my performance of flocked bird wings outstretched arms in the mirror or on film even in photographs,

Little Lina comes out and sits front row when it's my turn to perform.

Pink roses in her hands and braids in her hair, she had to improvise the morning routine in order to put them there.

To invent, compose, or perform with little or no

preparation I had to learn to improvise.

Out of the cleverness of God, in only desperate situations, I've learned to improvise.

When I couldn't figure out how to do THIS, I learned to do THAT Better!

Improvisation is our history, look at soul food. It used to be slop food.

Parts and pieces of no value except to the One who created it, intestines and carcasses from this and that.

Now the comfort of our country is food, no wonder we're all fat!

Fat with greed and pride and endless hunger a wanting for more…

I attest that improvisation ain't always so bad. Last I heard generic medications work just as well as name brand prescriptions at half the price…improvise.

Macellina found out it is a misconception that peacocks strut cuz they can't fly; oh, no sir! No ma'am! Peacocks indeed can fly, but because of the burden of such beautiful wings they were forced to improvise.

Little Lina slow danced with her first boyfriend, hand to hip, embraced her church group girlfriends and learned to smooth her deodorant.

Macellina A. Odd

She learned to tie her shoe,

And learned to sponge roll her own hair,

When the children of her sisters came, she learned

affectionate holding care…

It took improvisation to get her there.

I danced the club floors dusty

Exchanged my back-it-up shake for a sanctified two-step

Once afraid to expose both visible and invisible parts of me

I now breathe deep, close my eyes, and exalt Him freely

Arms wide open; tested to improvise.

Into Fruition

"Jesus wrap your arms around us like a blanket. Let us rest in your hands today, that this day has begun and will be made well. Let your wind guide us in our journeys. We pray for miracles, transparency, recovery and transformation on this new dawn day. In His name we pray, Amen."

—*Brittany Amonoo*

Into Fruition

Be...For...

This world will constantly define you, telling you who you are and what you ought to be...

Be YOU

Into Fruition

Be BRAVE...for bravery hibernates inside of you

Be STILL...for it is then that you hear the voice of the Lord guiding you

Be PATIENT...for then you will see the outcome of what once was impossible

Be OPEN...for that is the only way to love

Be GENTLE...for more words are heard that way

Be COURAGEOUS...for He is courageous

Be BOLD...for there is no greater way to live

Be HONEST...for liars are the worst of us all

Be READY...for your enemy always is

Be REGAL...for you are royal

Be Grateful...for everything

Be HOLY...for God is holy

Be ENOUGH...for you already are.

Be BEAUTIFUL...for you transcend the meaning of the word

Be FREE...for it was costly

Be GENEROUS...for the giver is the blesser

Be VULNERABLE...for your heart deserves to be heard

Be GRACEFUL...for it is captivating and undeserved

Into Fruition

"Your life is important. Your life matters. Everything you do in this life has a purpose and cannot and should not be dictated by anyone else."

—*Laryssa, 22*

What IF?

Into Fruition

What if you were the author...how would you define "Enough"?

What if today was your last...what would you do?

What if you weren't scared...what would you do?

What if money was no object...what would you do?

What if you hadn't gone through that...who would you be?

What if your life was described in one word...what would it be?

What if you weren't afraid...what would you say?

What if you get exactly what you want...what will you do next?

What if your heart was never broken...how would you love?

What if everyone was listening...what would you say?

What if no one ever found out...what would you do?

What if you had the chance...where would you go?

What if you wrote a song...what would you sing?

What if the drums began to play...how would you dance?

What if you weren't embarrassed...how would you behave?

What if your life was a movie...what would be the story?

What if we never meet...what would you want me to know?

Life is an ever changing, ever evolving event. Don't expect to ride the same ride over and over again. You will do yourself a terrible disservice missing out on some spectacular thrills!

Into Fruition

"Embrace the path given to you. Your path is different for a reason and should not be compared to anyone else's. God created yours to be special. Trust it."

—*Anonymous*

Enough

Into Fruition

You ARE enough.

You DO enough.

You HAVE enough.

You're SMART enough.

You're SUCCESSFUL enough.

You're VALUABLE enough.

You're PRETTY enough.

You are FIERCE enough.

Your ENOUGH is ENOUGH!!

The Journey through the Chrysalis

Into Fruition

It's not about rediscovering yourself
but accepting who God has created you to be
and accepting that a new season may bring about
a new you

Change is like the transmutation of only just realizing who
you are as you suddenly become someone you don't
recognize only to understand that you are who you were
meant to be all along

and all of the phases were the chapters of your book
It wasn't the end game that made the journey worth the ride
but the stretching and the growing that came about during
the process that made it worthwhile

—*Shontey Keys*

Six and Counting: Harriet Esi

Into Fruition

"Girl, I got my taxes back! I'm sending you the money for half your flight, come to Atlanta!"

What had I gotten myself into? There was never really any burning desire in me to visit Georgia, even the glitz and glamour of reality TV's portrayal of "Black Hollywood" didn't particularly lure me. In all honesty, I always thought I'd feel out of place as a petite Cali girl, used to farm-to-fork functions on the Sacramento River, amidst all that bodacious booty and southern hospitality.

"Okay cousin, why not? I better start my squats."

Southwest is treating me pretty well. The flight change in Denver proved itself entertaining. People-watching is a pastime that never gets old. The dark-haired white man in the baby blue dress shirt is taking extra-long glances in my direction and I can't help but wonder if he's intrigued by what he sees of my skin, or my hair, or my smile… or if he's reciting age old stereotypes he learned from his Pa and FOX News? His shoes are nice.

How on earth does she live twenty-three minutes away, yet I've been standing here waiting for seventy-one minutes? It's okay Maci, you're on vacation, relax.

"I'm so glad you made it, Cousin! Welcome to Atlanta! You for real just made my birthday weekend." The smell of medium-well-made cheeseburgers and vodka shots at the charming bar just down the street from Harriet's apartment eased my anxiety. "Me too, Cousin, I'm excited! Thanks for getting me here."

A Memorial Day weekend jam packed with parties, dinners, shopping, historically black college tours, MLK's birth home, jazz festivals and Carnival surely proved itself to be spectacular! And yes… the strip clubs that Atlanta, Georgia is notorious for proved themselves to live up to all the hype. Men in the south are even gentlemen in the strip club… The conversation regarding our parents, now that's what I wasn't looking forward to.

At the age of 31, in the middle of an unexpected divorce, I'm having an identity crisis. Have you ever lost sight of who the fuck you are? I don't know who the fuck I am anymore and now that I realize that, I also realize that I don't think I've ever known.

"Cousin, I feel so disconnected. I was volunteering as a leader at a youth retreat with a group of Nigerian ladies and they were all speaking their dialect, dancing, and making fun of their parent's thick accents, and there I was. I had nothing to say. I just watched, partly sad, partly in awe. Why is it that you feel such a strong sense of culture and pride about being Ghanaian? I've never had that. My dad never really taught us anything about being Ghanaian, like nothing. He didn't teach us the language because he didn't want it to 'mess up our English'. He made plantains but never jollof rice. The music is in my soul and I can't help but dance to the drums, but I don't know the history of the drumming or the names of the dances, not outside my ethnic studies classes anyway. Not for myself. It's not fair."

"Cousin," she looks at me from the driver's seat of her black Honda Accord. "...it's okay that you feel this way. You've been through a lot. For a long time, my mom was scared for me to go visit Home, she said things have changed so much, but I told her I was going to do it with or without her. When I left, she finally believed me. At some point you have to make up your mind for yourself."

I have no poker face. I used to get in trouble working in the mall at Macy's all the time when customers would say stupid shit to me. My facial expressions gave my every thought away. This car ride was no different. "What are you thinking?" she asked me.

"I'm thinking that I can't blame my dad anymore for not exposing us to our culture. At this point I'm hella grown and I have to take the responsibility for myself. If I want to know, I can find out for myself. My dad did the best he knew how at that time. Now it's up to me. But where do I even start?"

"Cousin, think of it this way, I grew up as a girl with a Ghanaian mother who taught me what it was like for her as a Ghanaian woman. Your mom is American; she taught you what it was like to grow up as a Black-American woman. What I have learned are a result of what women share in the culture. Your dad, being a man, was not able to share those things with you. Not because he didn't want to, but he couldn't. How could he have known to teach you about the meaning of waistbeads for example?"

I've seen Harriet's waistbeads a few times now and each time I catch a glimpse my eyes smile. Waistbeads date back centuries all over West Africa, but especially in Ghana. When a child is born the elders of a family will tie a string of tiny, intricate beads around the small child's waist. These beads grow tighter as the child gains weight, a great indicator that the child is healthy and growing properly. Once the male child reaches about five or six years old the beads are removed. For the girls, however, folklore has it that a girl begins her collection of adorning pieces as she hits milestones throughout her life; her first menstrual period, her wedding day, her pregnancy. These strands of beauty were, and still are, used to define a woman's waist and accentuate beauty. Traditional Ghanaian culture used the strings of the many strands around the bikini line as an anchor to strap the menstrual cloth. Waistbeads are a symbol of femininity and sensuality. Only the partner a woman chooses would have the honor of seeing them fully. A cross between jewelry and lingerie.

"Cousin, I can't believe a city like this exists! Black folks are thriving here! Why hasn't this been replicated all over the country?" For the first time in my life, I could see myself in everything. Every billboard, every cashier, the Whole Foods store was full of black folks! Like normal black folks! Not just the sectioned off sub-group that wears locs in their hair and consistently smell like the sweet cross of marijuana and incense. Every construction worker was black, all the businessmen and women walking around in Dockers and stilettos were black. The music was black, the art was black and the families... they were black. It was a dream to me.

The drive to Ike's Restaurant is at least thirty minutes and on the way is every shade of black excellence I have ever seen in my life. Awestruck only begins to describe my countenance.

We walked into Ike's and Ghanaian cuisine was obvious. The smell of ripened stewed tomatoes, coconut oil, fresh fish, cooked onions and peppers permeated the air long before the entrance. Adoja was our waitress; Adjoa, who shared the same name as I would have had if my Texarkana born and raised mother, been able to correctly pronounce it. Born on Monday, that's what it means in Fanti. Beautiful rich, dark chocolate Adjoa, whose smile lit brighter than August summers.

"We'll take the banku and tilapia, with jollof rice and peppers. Thank you." Harriet is a pro. She placed that order with only half looking at the menu and half sizing up the men gawking at her from the corner table. Amongst all this food was a clear bowl of warm water and lemons, "…you use that to clean your hands, that way the fish doesn't make your fingers stink." My face spoke the "aha" understanding for me.

Palm wine. We ordered palm wine. Now as much as I don't know about being Ghanaian, I do know that you gotta be awfully careful when you drink palm wine! "It's explosive!" my dad says. Created from the sap of various species of palm trees, the white liquid tends to be very sweet and non-alcoholic before it is fermented. Fermentation begins immediately after collection due to natural yeasts in the air. Within two hours, fermentation yields an aromatic wine, up to 4% alcohol content, mildly intoxicating and sweet. The longer it sits, the stronger it gets.

Finishing that meal and leaving that restaurant, I feel more African than I've ever felt in my life. I raised my chin a little higher, my back is a little straighter and I think I'm a little bit taller than when I walked in. Something in the fish perhaps? The drive back to Harriet's apartment seemed to be much shorter after leaving Ike's. Maybe my mind had simply wandered to a place that existed without time.

"Hey Cousin, I have something for you. Come here, turn around."

They felt amazing around my waist. These inconspicuous little beads perfectly fitted around these hips of mine that have entertained lovers but have yet to bear children. These tiny shimmers of pink and gold and blues that have now multiplied in numbers and variations; these stranded pieces of beauty and grace, indicators of growth and markers of history. These small threads which encircle me and remind me of the Ghanaian woman I am. Waistbeads, six and counting.

Into Fruition

"Don't be scared to take risks because you will never know the sort of outcome you'll receive. Live bravely and boldly in all choices."

—*Anonymous*

Into Fruition

To the love of my ENTIRE life, the man who has supported me through every step of this writing journey, the earthly reason this book finally got finished… Wayne Odd, you are EVERYTHING!!!

Blankets

Into Fruition

His covering was strewn over me, soft, warm, just the right amount of heavy; Unexpected. Brown, it smells like skin, clean and personal, pleasantly stenched somewhere between laundry two weeks ago and last night's cologne. His protection wrapped around me, the sweetness of chocolate and the safety of warm bath waters.

I don't want to leave this space. Engulf me in this blanket forever until forever lives outside of time. I am perfect here. Adored; cared for; spoken to with touches of sugar; kissed with the assurance of next time. I'm silly here, held in the paradise of captivity with broad shoulders and weight twice my own.

This blanket of mine flapping in the warm breeze of Sunday afternoons, in front of football games and white sauced pizza, is patience. Laughter is heard from beneath it, more like schoolgirl giggles from the most innocent of the bunch. Facial caresses of the soft fibers that make up this mighty shield feel like home. He feels like righteousness;

redemptive sheets as enormous as forest bears and roaring voices like beach ocean waves to match.

Honey spilled from his lips and set there in the twice colored cloth. My eyes fixed there for more than a moment, then without hesitation I savored that gooey goodness for fifty-three minutes and twenty-four seconds of my existence. How it stuck to me, messy and sincere resembling trust. He shelters me as gentle as hairline strokes away from the eyes, solid as deserted ground planting my feet, fluid as red wine pours, firm like summer nectarines.

This blanket of mine; novel; exhilarating; rousing; benign; lost is where I find myself in him. Keenly aware of what might be at any instant of any second; divine, vigilant, temperate, sensual in such pure ways; militant and stoic when on assignment. He searches me, diligently seeking the peace longed for. He finds me, waiting; diligently seeking peace I long for. His arms outstretched, long and wide welcoming me inside; his fabric dances and I fall apart, completely cloaked in this coffee painted cape. Daring to be consoled once again, aware of all possibilities attached to failure.

I've owned others, none so big, and none that ever felt quite so secure. None I wanted to keep as much as this.

I've owned others, none so big, and none that ever felt quite so secure. None I wanted to keep as much as this.

For My Love, Wayne J. Odd III
by Macellina Amonoo
2018

www.ingramcontent.com/pod-product-compliance
Lightning Source LLC
Chambersburg PA
CBHW062041290426
44109CB00026B/2692